ears that hear even better
bat

pointy ears
zebra

floppy ears
lop-eared bunny

soft ears
puppy

hard ears
armadillo

little ears
gorilla

very big ears
African elephant

P9-BZS-768

For my parents, with love and thanks—ST

Library of Congress Cataloging-in-Publication data is on file with the publisher.

Text copyright © 2019 by Sue Tarsky
Illustrations copyright © 2019 by Albert Whitman & Company
First published in the United States of America in 2019 by Albert Whitman & Company
ISBN 978-0-8075-9040-9

All rights reserved. No part of this book may be reproduced or transmitted in any
form or by any means, electronic or mechanical, including photocopying,
recording, or by any information storage and retrieval system,
without permission in writing from the publisher.

Printed in China
10 9 8 7 6 5 4 3 2 1 HH 22 21 20 19 18

Design by Aphee Messer

For more information about Albert Whitman & Company,
visit our website at www.albertwhitman.com.

100 Years of Albert Whitman & Company
Celebrate with us in 2019!

Whose Are These?

Whose Ears?

Sue Tarsky

Albert Whitman & Company
Chicago, Illinois

big ears

little ears

VERY big ears

VERY little ears

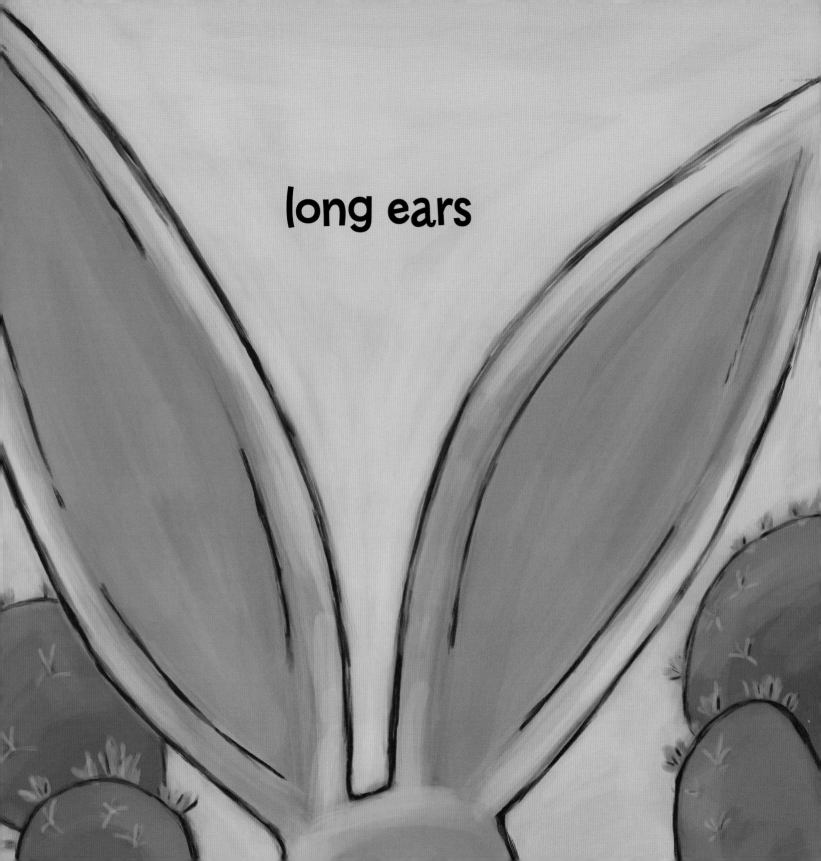

long ears

short ears

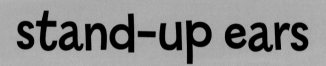

stand-up ears

floppy ears

ears that hear well

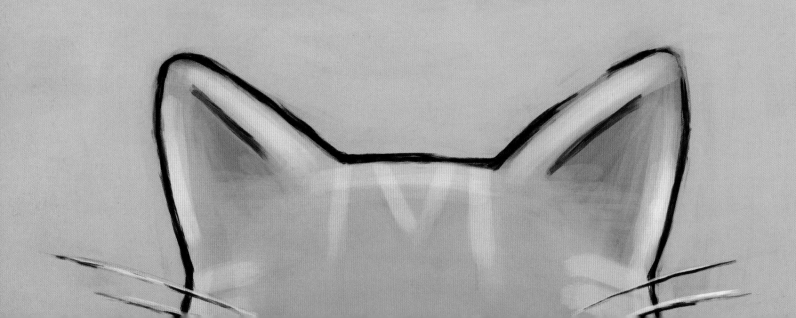

ears that hear even better

soft ears

hard ears

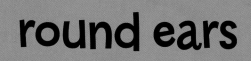

round ears

pointy ears

your ears

my ears!

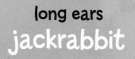

long ears
jackrabbit

round ears
panda

big ears
fox

short ears
short-eared owl

ears that hear well
cat

very small ears
beaver

stand-up ears
pony

31192021713993